Mommy's Little Helper Cookbook

by Karen Brown
illustrated by Glenn Quist

Meadowbrook Press
Distributed by Simon & Schuster
New York

Library of Congress Cataloging-in-Publication Data
Brown, Karen, 1952 Feb. 19-
    Mommy's little helper cookbook / Karen Brown.
        p.   cm.
    Summary: A collection of simple recipes for a variety of dishes including
"Microwave Applesauce," "Cheesy Spaghetti," and "Chocolate Chip Squares."
    ISBN 0-88166-346-8 (Meadowbrook)—ISBN 0-689-83072-6 (Simon & Schuster)
    1. Cookery—Juvenile literarture. [1. Cookery.] I. Title.
TX652.5 .B745 2000
641.5'123—dc21   99-053515
                                                          CIP

Editors: Liya Lev Oertel, Christine Zuchora-Walske
Proofreader: Nancy Baldrica
Production Manager: Joe Gagne
Desktop Publishing: Danielle White
Illustrations: Glenn Quist

Published by Meadowbrook Press, 5451 Smetana Drive, Minnetonka, MN
55343

www.meadowbrookpress.com

BOOK TRADE DISTRIBUTION by Simon & Schuster, a division of Simon and
Schuster, Inc., 1230 Avenue of the Americas, New York, NY 10020

04 03 02   10 9 8 7 6 5 4 3 2

Printed in the United States of America

DEDICATION

With much love
to my nieces and nephews,

Dunc and Tobin Fulton,
Jocelyn and Kendra Lancaster,
and Will and Gillian Marsh,

who love to cook with their moms.

ACKNOWLEDGMENTS

With gratitude to all my friends at
Meadowbrook Press, and special thanks
to Bruce Lansky, Christine Zuchora-Walske,
and Steve Linders for their creative and
professional efforts.

 CONTENTS

A NOTE TO MOMS

You and your young child can share quality time and create treasured memories with this collection of classic recipes for the beginning cook.

   The foods in *Mommy's Little Helper Cookbook* are simple, delicious, and appropriate for snacks or light meals. Every recipe is accompanied by helpful illustrations and divided into simple steps, each of which is marked clearly for mommy 👧 or child 😊. We suggest that you and your child read each recipe aloud before you begin and keep these tips in mind:

- Handle hot items with potholders or oven mitts to prevent burns.
- When cooking on the stove top, keep pan handles turned away from you to avoid bumping them and spilling hot ingredients.
- Never leave a child unsupervised around hot appliances.
- Put away sharp knives immediately after use.
- Do not allow a small child to operate an electric blender, hand mixer, or food processor. If you must use these appliances, do so ahead of time. Alternatively, you might let your child help by using a manual eggbeater or grater.
- Clean up as you go along and have plenty of towels on hand for spills.
- Do not allow children to taste batter or lick utensils if a mixture contains raw eggs.

The child's instructions for each recipe include basic tasks that most three- to seven-year-olds can handle with adult supervision: using measuring cups and spoons, counting out quantities, stirring batter, rolling dough, greasing pans, and garnishing dishes before serving. These tasks will help your child learn simple math and science concepts, practice following directions, and develop fine motor skills. Even more important than the skills your child will learn and practice is the feeling of accomplishment and confidence he or she will gain. Your child will be rightfully proud of the delicious dishes the two of you make together. Best of all, this book will help you cultivate a fun and fruitful relationship with your child.

So grab your aprons and get ready for a terrific time in the kitchen. With *Mommy's Little Helper Cookbook,* you'll cook up good food and great fun with your little one!

Enjoy,

Karen Brown

GOOD MORNING BREAKFAST

BANANA-ORANGE CUPS

Fresh-fruit lovers know that oranges and bananas are usually available all year long. So take advantage of their accessibility and combine them to make a fruit salad so good, you'll want it every day!

Makes: 2 cups

Ingredients:
- 2 large, ripe oranges
- 1 banana

Materials:
- Sharp knife (for slicing)
- Spoon
- Medium bowl

What to Do:

 1. Slice off tops of oranges and trim bottoms so the oranges will sit level.

 2. Break the banana into bite-size pieces.

 3. Scoop out the orange fruit and put in a bowl. Reserve the orange shells.

 4. Pick seeds out of the orange fruit if necessary.

5. Stir together orange fruit and bananas.

6. Spoon the fruit into the orange shells.

Creative Option:
Add 2 tablespoons sweetened, flaked coconut to the fruit mixture. It's delicious.

BLUEBERRY-BRAN MUFFINS

Get a sweet start on your day with these healthy, heavenly muffins.

Makes: 12 muffins

Ingredients:
- Vegetable-oil spray
- 2 eggs
- ½ cup oil
- 1 cup sugar
- 1 cup milk
- 1 cup flour
- 1 teaspoon baking soda
- ½ teaspoon salt
- ½ teaspoon vanilla extract
- 2½ cups bran flakes
- ½ cup blueberries

Materials:
- Oven
- Muffin tin
- 2 mixing bowls
- Measuring cup and spoons
- Whisk or fork
- Sifter
- Large spoon
- Oven mitts

What to Do:

 1. Preheat the oven to 400°F.

2. **Spray muffin tin with vegetable-oil spray.**

3. **In a bowl, mix eggs, oil, sugar, and milk with a whisk or fork.**

4. Sift together flour, baking soda, and salt and add to the egg mixture.

5. Add vanilla and fold in the bran flakes and blueberries.

6. Spoon the batter into the muffin tin.

7. Use oven mitts to place the muffin tin in the hot oven. Bake for 15 minutes.

8. Eat warm or cold!

Creative Option:
Try raisins instead of blueberries for delicious raisin-bran treats.

CHEESY DROP BISCUITS

Biscuits are fun to make—and messy! You may need an apron for this recipe, or wear a big old shirt to protect your clothes. Just roll up the sleeves and dig in!

Makes: 24 biscuits

Ingredients:
- 2 cups all-purpose flour
- 3 teaspoons baking powder
- 1 teaspoon salt
- ⅓ cup shortening
- 1 cup milk
- 1 cup grated Cheddar cheese
- Vegetable-oil spray

Materials:
- Oven
- Sifter
- Large mixing bowl
- Measuring cups and spoons
- Pastry blender or 2 knives
- Mixing spoons
- Cookie sheet
- Oven mitts

What to Do:

 1. Preheat the oven to 450°F.

 2. **Sift together flour, baking powder, and salt into a large mixing bowl.**

 3. Use a pastry blender or 2 knives to cut shortening into the flour mixture. Blend until crumbly.

 4. **Add milk and cheese.**

5. Stir with a spoon until the batter is well mixed.

 6. Spray a cookie sheet with vegetable-oil spray.

 7. Use a tablespoon to drop batter onto the cookie sheet.

 8. Use oven mitts to place the cookie sheet in the hot oven. Bake for 10 minutes or until golden brown.

 9. Eat warm with butter and honey.

Creative Option:
For biscuits that are even more savory, stir ½ cup bacon bits into the batter.

CHOCOLATE CRESCENTS

You'll lick your fingers—and the plate—after eating these terrific rolls filled with melted chocolate. Some kids think these are the best rolls ever; try them and see!

Makes: 8 rolls

Ingredients:
- 1 8-ounce can refrigerated crescent roll dough
- ½ cup chocolate chips

Materials:
- Oven
- Cookie sheet
- Measuring cups and spoons
- Oven mitts

What to Do:

 1. Preheat the oven to 375°F. Open the can of dough.

2. Separate the dough triangles.

3. Arrange the dough triangles on an ungreased cookie sheet.

4. Place 1 tablespoon of chocolate chips in the center of each triangle.

 6. Use oven mitts to place the cookie sheet in the hot oven. Bake for about 12 minutes, or until golden.

 7. Let the rolls cool before you gobble them up.

5. Roll up the triangles into crescents, starting with one side and rolling toward the point.

Creative Option:
Sprinkle powdered sugar on top of the just-baked rolls for a real bakery look.

CINNAMON TOAST

Don't you just love the cozy taste of cinnamon toast? The best thing about it is how quick and easy it is to make! Here's to a toasty and tasty breakfast treat.

Makes: 2 slices

Ingredients:
- 2 slices bread
- 2 teaspoons butter or margarine, softened
- ½ teaspoon cinnamon
- 2 teaspoons granulated sugar

Materials:
- Oven
- Cookie sheet
- Oven mitts
- Spatula
- Butter knife (for spreading)
- Measuring spoons
- Small bowl

What to Do:

 1. Preheat the oven broiler.

 2. Place bread on a cookie sheet.

 3. Use oven mitts to place the cookie sheet under the broiler and leave the oven door open. When the toast is brown, remove the cookie sheet from the oven.

 4. Turn the bread over with a spatula and spread butter on the unbrowned sides. (Careful, the pan is hot!)

 5. Combine cinnamon and sugar in a small bowl.

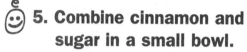

 6. Sprinkle the cinnamon mixture over the buttered sides of the bread.

7. Return the bread to the broiler and toast for 1–2 minutes.

 8. Let the toast cool a bit before you eat it, or you'll burn your mouth!

Creative Option:
Use brown sugar instead of granulated sugar for a sweeter taste.

FRENCH TOAST

W hat's better than French toast for breakfast? French toast for supper! This awesome dish is an excellent way to start the day—or finish it. Ready, set, go!

Makes: 4 toasts

Ingredients:
- 1 egg
- ½ cup milk
- 4 slices bread
- Vegetable-oil spray
- Syrup or jam

Materials:
- Small mixing bowl
- Whisk or fork
- Measuring cups
- Shallow pan
- Skillet
- Stove
- Spatula

What to Do:

1. Break an egg into a bowl.

2. Beat the egg with a whisk or fork until the egg is frothy.

3. Add milk to the egg.

4. Pour the mixture into a shallow pan.

 5. Place the bread side by side in the egg-and-milk mixture; let soak for 2 minutes on each side.

 6. Spray a skillet with vegetable-oil spray.

 7. Place the skillet on the stove, and turn the heat to medium.

 8. Use a large spatula to lift the soaked bread into the skillet. (Careful, the pan will be hot!)

 9. Fry for 2 minutes on each side, or until golden brown.

 10. Top with syrup or jam and dig in!

Creative Option:
Sprinkle with powdered sugar and garnish with your favorite fresh berries.

FRUIT WITH YOGURT DIP

Strawberries are good . . . and melon is very tasty. Of course, grapes are great, too. Can't decide which fruit is your favorite? That's okay—you don't have to! Simply whip up a batch of this yummy yogurt dip, and eat it with all your favorite fruits.

Makes: 2–4 servings

Ingredients:
- 1 4-ounce package frozen strawberries, thawed
- 1 cup lemon yogurt
- 1 cup fresh strawberry pieces
- 1 cup melon chunks
- 1 cup seedless grapes

Materials:
- Large mixing bowl
- Measuring cups
- Blender or whisk
- Serving plate
- Spoon
- Small serving bowl

What to Do:

1. Pour thawed strawberries into a large mixing bowl.

2. Add lemon yogurt to the strawberries.

 3. Use a blender or whisk to combine yogurt and frozen strawberries until well blended.

 4. **Arrange fresh fruit on a serving plate, leaving the middle empty.**

 5. **Spoon the dip into a small serving bowl and place the bowl in the middle of the serving plate.**

 6. **Go for a dip!**

Creative Option:
Try dipping other fresh fruit, such as pineapple, apple, or pear slices.

MICROWAVE APPLESAUCE

Have you ever made your own applesauce? You'll be amazed at how easy and delicious it is. Besides, homemade applesauce is really fun to make; there's lots of mixing and mashing!

Makes: 2–3 servings

Ingredients:
- 4 large apples
- ¼ cup water
- 1 tablespoon lemon juice
- 2 tablespoons honey
- Cinnamon to taste

Materials:
- Paring knife
- Microwave-safe bowl
- Measuring cups and spoons
- Large spoon
- Microwave
- Potato masher
- 2–3 serving dishes
- 2–3 spoons

What to Do:

 1. Peel apples and slice into large chunks. Place apple chunks in a microwave-safe bowl.

 2. **Pour water over the apples.**

 3. **Add lemon juice and honey.**

4. Stir the mixture to coat the apples well.

 5. Cover the bowl and place in the microwave. Cook 4 minutes on high. Check the apples; if they are not yet mushy, cook for another minute.

 6. Use a potato masher to smash the apples into a purée.

 7. Spoon applesauce into serving dishes.

 8. Sprinkle each serving with cinnamon and eat warm or chilled.

Creative Option:
Use the applesauce as a topping for pancakes or oatmeal when you're feeling adventurous!

OATMEAL WITH RAISINS

What's more heartwarming —and tummy warming— than oatmeal? It's one of the best breakfast foods to help you get up and go in the morning. So get up and go to it!

Makes: 2 servings

Ingredients:
- 2 cups water
- ½ teaspoon salt
- 1 cup rolled oats
- ½ cup raisins
- Sugar to taste
- Milk or cream to taste

Materials:
- Measuring cups and spoons
- Medium saucepan
- Stove
- Spoon
- 2 serving bowls

What to Do:

 1. Pour water into a medium saucepan.

 2. Bring water to a boil over medium-high heat.

 3. Add salt to boiling water.

 4. Carefully stir oats into the boiling water.

5. Carefully stir raisins into the oats.

6. Turn heat to low and stir the oatmeal for 5 minutes until it's creamy.

7. Spoon the hot oatmeal into serving bowls.

8. **Sprinkle with sugar and add milk or cream.**

Creative Options:

Oatmeal is not just for breakfast. Why not try it on a cold winter night for supper, too?

For a different flavor, use brown sugar instead of white and stir in fresh sliced apples.

PERFECT PANCAKES

Pancakes for breakfast? Yum! These perfect pancakes will really wake you up. You'll like them so much, you'll want seconds.

Makes: 8 pancakes

Ingredients:
- 1 egg
- 1 cup milk
- 1 tablespoon vegetable oil
- 1½ cups all-purpose flour
- 2 teaspoons baking powder
- ½ teaspoon salt
- Vegetable-oil spray
- Butter and syrup

Materials:
- 2 mixing bowls
- Fork or whisk
- Large spoon
- Sifter
- Stove
- Griddle or skillet
- Spatula

What to Do:

1. Break an egg into a small mixing bowl.

2. Beat the egg with a whisk or fork until frothy.

3. Stir milk and oil into the beaten egg.

4. In a medium bowl, sift together flour, baking powder and salt.

 5. Stir the flour mixture into the egg mixture.

 8. Place the griddle on the stove and allow it to heat up.

 9. Carefully pour ¼ cup of batter onto the hot griddle. Repeat with the rest of the batter. When bubbles form on top of the pancakes and the edges turn brown, use a spatula to flip them. Cook until golden brown.

 10. Top with butter and syrup.

Creative Options:
For variety, make little pancakes (called silver-dollar pancakes) or cut out almost-done pancakes with a favorite cookie cutter.

 6. Turn the stove on medium heat.

 7. Spray the griddle or skillet with vegetable-oil spray.

QUICK CINNAMON ROLLS

You'll want to fill up on these sticky, gooey cinnamon rolls. When you reach for seconds, just say they're not as good when they're cold!

Makes: 10 cinnamon rolls

Ingredients:
- Vegetable-oil spray
- ½ cup butter, melted
- ½ cup sugar
- 1 tablespoon cinnamon
- 1 7½-ounce can refrigerated biscuit dough

Materials:
- Oven
- Round cake pan
- Measuring cups and spoons
- Small bowl
- Fork or spoon
- Oven mitts

What to Do:

 1. Preheat the oven to 425°F.

2. **Spray a round cake pan with vegetable-oil spray.**

3. **Combine melted butter, sugar, and cinnamon in a small bowl; mix with a fork or spoon.**

4. Roll each raw biscuit in the sugar mixture and place in the pan.

5. Use oven mitts to place the pan in the hot oven. Bake 10–12 minutes.

6. Lick your fingers while eating!

Creative Option:
Press raisins into each biscuit before baking.

RAISIN-BREAD PEOPLE

You'll put a happy face on your morning with this project. Have fun creating your own little breakfast people— and serving up smiles all around!

Makes: 2 servings

Ingredients:
- 2 slices raisin bread
- 2 tablespoons cream cheese, softened
- Chopped nuts
- Chopped maraschino cherries
- Raisins

Materials:
- Cutting board
- Person-shaped cookie cutter
- Knife (for spreading)
- Measuring spoons

What to Do:

1. Lay the bread slices on a cutting board.

2. Cut each slice with a person-shaped cookie cutter.

3. Spread a thin layer of cream cheese on top of each raisin-bread person.

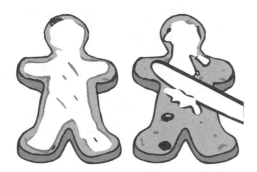

4. Press in nuts, cherries, and raisins to create faces and buttons.

Creative Option:
If you prefer, use peanut butter instead of cream cheese.

SCRAMBLED-EGG SURPRISE

Mmm! When you wake up hungry enough to eat a horse, try these scrambled eggs. There's nothing like the aroma of eggs cooking in the morning!

Makes: 2 servings

Ingredients:
- 3 eggs
- 2 tablespoons cold water
- Salt and pepper to taste
- 1 tablespoon butter or margarine
- ¼ cup bacon bits

Materials:
- Mixing bowl
- Measuring spoons and cups
- Whisk or fork
- Stove
- Small skillet
- 2 serving plates
- Large spoon

What to Do:

1. Break eggs into a mixing bowl.

2. Add water, salt, and pepper to the eggs.

3. Beat the eggs with a whisk or a fork until frothy.

4. Heat a small skillet over medium-low heat.

 5. **Drop butter or margarine into the skillet and wait for it to melt.**

 8. Continue to cook and st the eggs for a few more minutes, until they are no longer runny.

 9. **Get two plates ready and spoon the eggs onto the plates.**

 6. Pour the egg mixture into the hot skillet and let it cook for about a minute.

 7. **Sprinkle bacon bits over the cooking eggs.**

Creative Option:
Eggs-periment by adding diced ham or grated cheese during Step 7.

ANYTIME SNACKS

BANANA BITES

Go bananas over this fun recipe! Roll, dip, and eat, then lick your fingers!

Makes: about 12 small treats

Ingredients:
- 2 bananas
- ¼ cup chopped nuts
- ½ cup rolled oats
- ¼ cup honey

Materials:
- Large bowl
- Measuring cups
- Small bowl
- Tray
- Aluminum foil
- Freezer

What to Do:

 1. Peel and break bananas into 1-inch chunks.

 2. In a large bowl, mix together nuts and oats.

3. Pour honey into a small bowl.

 4. Dip bananas in honey, then roll them in the oat mixture.

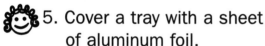

 5. Cover a tray with a sheet of aluminum foil.

 6. Place the coated banana chunks on the tray.

 7. Freeze the banana bites for at least 1 hour. Before serving, thaw them for a few minutes so they are not so hard and cold.

 8. Pop one in your mouth!

Creative Option: Insert small sticks into the banana chunks before coating to make frozen banana pops!

FRUIT-LEATHER ROLLS

These fruit-leather rolls take a long time to cook, but are sure worth the wait! Don't just twiddle your thumbs while they cook—share a hug or a story —or both!

Makes: about 24 rolls

Ingredients:
- Vegetable-oil spray
- 3 cups canned peaches or pears, drained
- 2 tablespoons honey
- 1 tablespoon lemon juice

Materials:
- Oven
- Cookie sheet
- Measuring cups and spoons
- Blender
- Spatula
- Scissors
- Oven mitts

What to Do:

 1. Preheat the oven to 200°F.

2. Spray a cookie sheet with vegetable-oil spray.

3. Place fruit, honey, and lemon juice in a blender.

4. Purée the mixture until smooth.

5. Pour the fruit purée onto the cookie sheet.

 8. When dry and cool (after several hours), cut the leather into thin strips with scissors.

 9. Place each strip on a piece of plastic wrap and roll it up for safe-keeping until you are ready to eat it.

6. Use a spatula to spread the fruit purée evenly across the pan.

Creative Option:
Make extra rolls and tie them up with ribbons to give to your friends!

7. Use oven mitts to place the cookie sheet in the hot oven. Bake for 2 hours, turn, then bake 1 more hour.

FRUITY FREEZER POPS

Make your own frozen fruit pops. Experiment with different kinds of fruit to see which ones you like best. These pops are tops!

Makes: 12 to 14 pops

Ingredients:
- 1 16-ounce can of fruit with natural juice

Materials:
- Blender
- Ice-cube tray
- Freezer
- Small wooden or plastic sticks

What to Do:

 1. Open a can of fruit in natural juice.

 2. **Pour the fruit and its juice into a blender.**

 3. Purée the fruit in the blender until smooth.

4. **Pour the fruit purée into an ice-cube tray.**

 5. Freeze the purée for 1 hour, until firm, but not solid.

 6. **Insert a small stick into each partly frozen cube.**

 7. Return the purée to the freezer until solid.

 8. **Remove a pop from the tray and lick away!**

Creative Options:
Freeze the fruit purée in small paper cups, then just peel away the cups and eat!

Place a cherry or blueberry in each cube before freezing to provide a fun surprise center.

NUTTY POPCORN BALLS

If you like popcorn, you'll love this swell snack. You'll love making it, too—you get to dig into gooey stuff. Remember to wash your hands first, then have fun!

Makes: about 12 popcorn balls

Ingredients:
- 3 cups miniature marsh-mallows
- 5 cups popped popcorn
- ½ cup peanuts
- 2 tablespoons butter or margarine, melted
- Extra butter for hands

Materials:
- Microwave-safe bowl
- Measuring cups and spoons
- Microwave
- 2 mixing bowls
- Oven mitts
- Wax paper

What to Do:

 1. **Place marshmallows in a microwave-safe bowl.**

 2. Cover the bowl, place it in the microwave, and heat the marshmallows for 2 minutes on high to melt them.

3. Using oven mitts, re-move the bowl from the microwave.

4. Pour popcorn into a large mixing bowl.

  7. Pour the melted marsh-mallows over the popcorn mixture. Cool slightly.

 8. Spread butter or margarine on your hands and shape the popcorn mixture into balls. Place the balls on a sheet of wax paper to cool.

 5. Pour melted butter or margarine over the popcorn.

 6. Add peanuts to the popcorn.

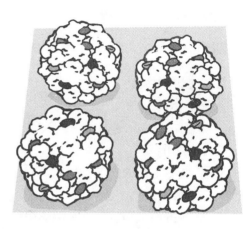

Creative Options:

Add ½ cup chocolate chips or candy bits to the popcorn mixture for added color and taste.

Try shaping the popcorn mixture into a variety of shapes.

For fun, add a few drops of food coloring to the popcorn mixture.

ORANGE GELATIN SQUARES

What's best thing about eating these gelatin squares? You get to play with your food! Any way you slice it, this treat is sure to please!

Makes: about 24 squares

Ingredients:
- 2½ cups orange juice
- 4 envelopes unflavored gelatin
- ½ cup sugar
- ¼ teaspoon salt
- 1 6-ounce can mandarin oranges, drained

Materials:
- Measuring cups and spoons
- Microwave-safe bowl
- Microwave
- Oven mitts
- Large spoon
- 9-by-13-inch baking pan
- Refrigerator
- Butter knife (for cutting)

What to Do:

 1. Pour orange juice into a microwave-safe bowl.

2. Cover the bowl, place it in the microwave, and heat the juice for 2 minutes on high. Check the juice. If it is not boiling, heat it for another minute. Using oven mitts, remove the bowl from the microwave.

3. **Stir gelatin, sugar, and salt into the hot juice.**

 4. **Stir in mandarin oranges.**

5. **Pour the gelatin mixture into a baking pan.**

 6. Place the pan in the refrigerator. Chill the gelatin for about 3–4 hours or until firm.

 7. **After the gelatin is firm, use a butter knife to cut it into squares.**

Creative Option:
Instead of making squares, use cookie cutters to create your favorite shapes.

PEANUT-BUTTER-AND-BANANA CONES

Did you think cones were only for ice cream? Certainly not! This recipe will teach you how to scoop up peanut butter and bananas for a different—and delicious—treat. You'll love it!

Makes: 2 cones

Ingredients:
- 1 ripe banana
- 2 tablespoons honey
- 4 tablespoons peanut butter
- 2 large waffle cones

Materials:
- Mixing bowl
- Measuring spoons
- Large spoon

What to Do:

1. Break a banana into bite-size chunks.

2. Measure honey and peanut butter into a bowl and mix well.

 3. Add banana chunks to the honey and peanut butter and mix well.

4. Spoon the mixture into waffle cones.

Creative Option:
Sprinkle granola on top for extra crunch!

PEANUT-BUTTER BALLS

Good things come in small packages. You can prove it with these tiny but terrific treats. Make a bunch—you'll want to share!

Makes: 24 balls

Ingredients:
- 1 cup peanut butter
- ½ cup nonfat powdered milk
- ¼ cup honey
- ½ teaspoon vanilla extract
- ½ cup finely ground pecans

Materials:
- Mixing bowl
- Measuring cups and spoons
- Fork
- Shallow bowl
- Tray
- Wax paper
- Refrigerator
- Serving tray or plate

What to Do:

 1. In a mixing bowl, stir together peanut butter, powdered milk, honey, and vanilla with a fork until well blended.

2. Pinch off small pieces of dough and roll into 1-inch balls.

3. Pour ground pecans into a shallow bowl.

  4. Roll balls in nuts until well coated.

5. Line a tray with a sheet of wax paper.

6. Place the peanut-butter balls on the tray.

 7. Chill the peanut-butter balls in the refrigerator for 30 minutes.

 8. Transfer the firm, chilled balls to a serving tray or plate.

Creative Option:
Instead of rolling the balls in ground nuts, try healthy, crunchy wheat germ!

PEAR BUNNIES

You can create magic with a few pieces of fruit. Just follow these directions and—voilà!—a rabbit will appear on your salad plate!

Makes: 2 bunnies

Ingredients:
- 2 large lettuce leaves
- 2 pear halves
- 2 maraschino cherries
- 4 raisins
- 4 slices water chestnuts
- ½ cup cottage cheese

Materials:
- 2 salad plates
- Ice-cream scoop

What to Do:

 1. Gather all ingredients on the counter.

 2. Place a lettuce leaf on each salad plate.

3. Place a pear half, rounded side up, on each lettuce leaf.

4. On the thin end of each pear, place a cherry for a nose, raisins for eyes, and water chestnuts sticking up for ears.

5. Place a scoop of cottage cheese at the fat end of each pear to make a tail.

6. Decide where to dig in first!

Creative Options:
Use a scoop of lemon yogurt for a tail or a cinnamon candy for a nose. Yum!

PICNIC EGGS

Chill out with these yummy deviled eggs. It's no yolk: Whether your picnic is outdoors or at your kitchen table, this is the perfect treat.

Makes: 8 egg halves

Ingredients:
- 4 eggs
- Water
- 1 heaping tablespoon mayonnaise
- ½ teaspoon prepared mustard
- ¼ teaspoon salt
- ¼ teaspoon pepper
- Dash of paprika

Materials:
- Small saucepan and cover
- Stove
- Paper towel
- Knife (for slicing)
- Measuring spoons
- Small bowl
- Fork

What to Do:

 1. **Place eggs in a small saucepan and cover them with water.**

 2. Bring the water to a boil, then cover the saucepan and remove from heat. Let stand for 15 minutes, then run eggs under cold water to cool them.

 3. **Peel shells from eggs, rinse, and dry.**

4. Slice each egg in half lengthwise. Use a teaspoon to remove the yolk from each egg half. Place the yolks in a small bowl.

 5. Mash the yolks with a fork.

6. Add mayonnaise, mustard, salt, and pepper. Mix well.

 7. Scoop the yolk mixture back into the egg whites.

8. Sprinkle each half with paprika.

Creative Option:
Try adding bacon bits or chopped ham to the yolk mixture. It's tasty!

PIGS IN BLANKETS

It's easy to make a pig of yourself with these fast and fun biscuit-wrapped franks. For lunch, after school, or as a late-morning snack—you'll say, "More, please!"

Makes: 10 snacks

Ingredients:
- 1 can (10-count) refrigerated biscuits
- 5 frankfurters
- Mustard
- Ketchup

Materials:
- Oven
- Knife (for slicing)
- Cookie sheet
- Oven mitts

What to Do:

 1. Preheat the oven to 400°F.

 2. Separate the biscuit dough into individual biscuits.

 3. Cut each frankfurter in half to get two short franks.

 4. Wrap biscuit dough around each frank half and place on an ungreased cookie sheet.

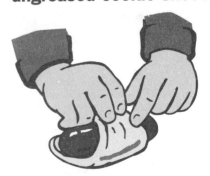

 5. Use oven mitts to place the cookie sheet in the hot oven. Bake for 10 minutes or until buscuits turn golden brown.

 6. Keep an eye on the biscuits to make sure they do not burn.

 7. Use oven mitts to remove the cookie sheet from the oven. Allow the pigs in blankets to cool for a few minutes.

 8. Dip the pigs in mustard and ketchup before gobbling them up.

Creative Option:
Wrap each frank half with a slice of American cheese inside the biscuit dough. Yum!

QUESO DIP AND CHIPS

When you need a quick snack, try this microwaved cheese dip with your favorite chips. It's fast and fabulous!

Makes: 2 to 3 servings

Ingredients:
- 8 ounces pasteurized process cheese
- 2 tablespoons milk
- ¼ cup salsa
- Tortilla chips

Materials:
- Knife (for slicing)
- Microwave-safe bowl
- Measuring cups and spoons
- Microwave
- Oven mitts
- Large spoon
- Serving tray
- Serving bowl

What to Do:

 1. Slice cheese into cubes and place in a microwave-safe bowl.

 2. Pour milk over the cheese.

 3. Cover the bowl, place it in the microwave, and cook for 1½ minutes on high.

 4. Check the mixture; if the cheese is not melted, cook for another 30 seconds on high. Use oven mitts to remove the bowl from the microwave.

5. Add salsa to the cheese mixture and stir.

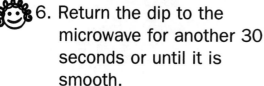6. Return the dip to the microwave for another 30 seconds or until it is smooth.

7. Arrange chips on a serving tray, leaving the center empty.

8. Transfer the hot dip into a serving bowl.

9. Use oven mitts to place the bowl of dip in the middle of the chips.

10. Dig in!

Creative Option:
Add chopped onions or black olives to the dip for extra zip.

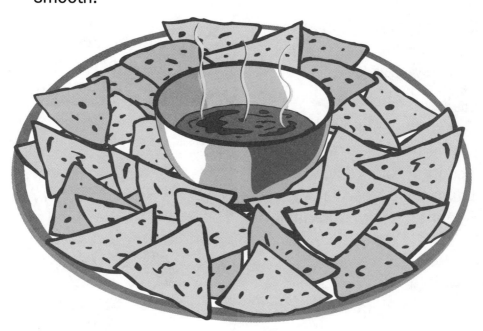

STUFFED CELERY

Score big with this quick and healthy snack. Celery is good with just about any kind of filling, and this veggie spread is especially delicious. Get ready to crunch and munch!

Makes: 4 stuffed celery stalks

Ingredients:
- ½ cup cream cheese
- 2 tablespoons shredded carrot
- 2 tablespoons chopped olives
- 4 celery stalks

Materials:
- Measuring cups and spoons
- Mixing bowl
- Spoon or fork
- Sharp knife (for slicing)
- Butter knife (for spreading)

What to Do:

1. Place cream cheese into a mixing bowl and mash with a spoon or fork until soft.

2. Add shredded carrots and chopped olives and mix until smooth.

 3. If you like, cut celery stalks in half for easier handling.

 4. Spread the cream-cheese mixture onto the celery stalks.

 5. Do your best rabbit impersonation and nibble away!

Creative Option:
You can save time by using a prepared cream cheese, already mixed with vegetables, pineapple, or strawberry.

TRAIL MIX

All kinds of yummy munchies go into this terrific trail mix. You will have a great time mixing it and an even better time eating it. Grab a handful!

Makes: 3½ cups of snack mix

Ingredients:
- 1 cup thin pretzel sticks
- ½ cup salted peanuts
- 2 tablespoons butter
- 1 cup round oat cereal (like Cheerios)
- 1 cup square wheat cereal (like Wheat Chex)
- ½ teaspoon Worcestershire sauce
- ¼ teaspoon garlic salt

Materials:
- Oven
- Measuring cups and spoons
- Microwave-safe bowl
- Microwave
- Large baking dish
- Large spoon
- Oven mitts

What to Do:

 1. Preheat the oven to 275°F.

 2. **Put pretzels, peanuts, and butter in a microwave-safe bowl.**

3. Cover the bowl and heat it in the microwave for 60 seconds on high.

4. **In a large baking dish, combine cereals, Worcestershire sauce, and garlic salt.**

 5. Use oven mitts to pour the hot, buttery pretzel mixture over the cereal mixture.

 6. **Mix everything well and spread evenly over the bottom of the baking dish.**

 7. Use oven mitts to place the baking dish in the hot oven. Bake for 30 minutes, stirring once or twice.

 8. **Let the trail mix cool, then grab a handful!**

Creative Option:
If you like, add dried fruit to the trail mix after cooking.

VEGGIES AND DIP

Pick the prettiest, freshest veggies at the grocery store, then serve them—crisp and cool—with this creamy dip. Go ahead and fill up on this super-scrumptious snack, because it's super-nutritious, too!

Makes: 2 cups dip

Ingredients:
- Carrots
- Celery
- Cucumbers
- Cherry tomatoes
- Broccoli
- Cauliflower
- 1 cup sour cream
- ½ cup mayonnaise
- 1 package dry onion dip mix

Materials:
- Sharp knife (for chopping)
- Mixing bowl
- Spoon
- Serving bowl
- Serving tray

What to Do:

1. Chop the vegetables into bite-size slices, sticks, and chunks.

2. **Put sour cream and mayonnaise into a mixing bowl.**

3. **Add dry onion dip and blend well.**

4. Transfer the dip to a serving bowl.

5. Arrange veggies on a serving tray, leaving the center empty for the dip.

6. Place the bowl of dip in the center of the veggies and sample your creation!

Creative Option:
For a quicker veggie fix, use your favorite ranch dressing as a dip.

YUMMY TEATIME CRACKERS

These snacks are pretty to look at and fun to eat! Serve them on a tray lined with a pretty paper doily.

Makes: as many as you want

Ingredients:
- Snack crackers
- Cheddar cheese and apple slices
- Cream cheese and raisins
- Pimiento cheese and green-pepper slices
- Dilled mustard and cucumber slices

Materials:
- Fancy tray
- Butter knife (for spreading)
- Paper doily

What to Do:

 1. Assemble the ingredients of your choice.

2. Place crackers on a fancy tray and top them with your favorite ingredients.

 3. Raise your pinkies in the air and have a party.

Creative Option:
Use rice cakes instead of crackers—they're bigger!

LOTS OF LUNCH

CARROT-CHEESE-APPLE ROLLUPS

Crunchy carrots, juicy apples, and savory cheese. What could be better than wrapping these all up together in a delicious tortilla? These rollups are great for a lunch box, a picnic, or an after-nap snack.

Makes: 2 rollups

Ingredients:
- ¼ cup grated carrot
- ¼ cup grated cheese
- ½ cup grated apple
- 1 tablespoon honey
- 2 large tortillas

Materials:
- Mixing bowl
- Measuring cups and spoons
- Large spoon
- Plastic wrap
- Refrigerator

What to Do:

1. In a mixing bowl, stir together carrot, cheese, apple, and honey.

2. Lay tortillas out flat.

3. Spoon filling onto one end of each tortilla, and roll up into cylinders.

5. Remove the plastic wrap and savor the flavor!

Creative Option:
Use tortillas instead of bread for all your favorite sandwiches. You can make peanut-butter-and-jelly rollups, bacon-lettuce-and-tomato rollups, or any other kind of rollup you want!

4. Wrap the rollups tightly in plastic wrap and refrigerate for at least 20 minutes.

CHEESY SPAGHETTI

Can you guess what makes this spaghetti special? It's served in a bowl lined with cheese!

Makes: 2 servings

Ingredients:
- ½ cup prepared spaghetti sauce
- 4 large squares mozzarella cheese
- 2 ounces cooked spaghetti
- 2 tablespoons grated Parmesan cheese

Materials:
- Measuring cups and spoons
- Small saucepan
- Stove
- Cutting board
- Sharp knife (for slicing)
- 2 serving bowls
- Large spoon

What to Do:

 1. Pour spaghetti sauce into a small saucepan and heat until warm.

 2. **Lay mozzarella squares flat on the cutting board.**

 3. Cut each slice diagonally into two triangles.

 4. **Place 4 cheese triangles points up around the inside of each bowl.**

 5. Spoon warm spaghetti
into the bowls.

 6. Spoon warm sauce over
the spaghetti.

 7. Sprinkle with Parmesan
cheese!

Creative Option:
Use any kind of pasta: mac-
aroni, bow-tie, or whatever
else strikes your fancy!

CRUNCHY SALAD

In a crunch for a delicious lunch? Fresh from the garden or the grocery store, this crisp, cool salad is good anytime. You'll agree—it's chillin'!

Makes: 2 servings

Ingredients:
- 1 cup shredded lettuce
- ¼ cup chopped green pepper
- ¼ cup chopped carrots
- ½ cup cheese cubes
- 2 tablespoons salad dressing
- Salt and pepper to taste

Materials:
- Large salad bowl
- Measuring cups and spoons
- Large fork and spoon (for tossing)
- 2 small salad bowls

What to Do:

 1. Place the vegetables and cheese cubes in a large salad bowl.

2. Pour salad dressing on top.

3. Toss the salad to mix well.

4. Divide the salad between two salad bowls.

5. Sprinkle salads with salt and pepper.

Creative Option:
Chop everything in large pieces, use the dressing as a dip, and turn this salad into finger food!

ENGLISH-MUFFIN PIZZAS

Wow, pizzas for lunch! What more could a kid ask for? You can make these amazing treats in minutes, and you'll eat 'em up in seconds!

Makes: as much as you want (2 muffin halves per serving)

Ingredients:
- English muffins, split into halves
- 1 jar pizza or spaghetti sauce
- Mozzarella cheese, grated
- Pepperoni slices
- Green-pepper slices

Materials:
- Oven
- Cookie sheet
- Large spoon
- Oven mitts

What to Do:

 1. Preheat the oven to 375°F.

2. **Place muffin halves on a cookie sheet.**

3. **Spoon some sauce onto each muffin half.**

4. Sprinkle some grated cheese over the sauce.

 7. Use oven mitts to place the pizzas in the hot oven. Bake for 10 minutes or until cheese is bubbly. Use oven mitts to remove pizzas from the oven.

 8. Let the pizzas cool slightly before eating.

5. Lay pepperoni slices on top of the cheese.

Creative Option:
Add chopped mushrooms, olives, or other veggies—pile on the toppings!

6. Place green pepper slices on the pepperoni.

GRILLED CHEESE SANDWICH

What's the all-time kids' lunch favorite? Grilled cheese, of course! It's so gooey and good, you just might have to eat two!

Makes: 1 sandwich

Ingredients:
- 2 slices bread
- 2 slices American cheese
- 1 tablespoon soft margarine

Materials:
- Skillet
- Stove
- Butter knife (for spreading)
- Measuring spoons
- Spatula

What to Do:

 1. Heat skillet over medium-low burner.

2. Place cheese slices on top of one bread slice.

3. Top with the second bread slice.

 4. Spread a thin layer of margarine on the outer sides of the sandwich.

 5. Place the sandwich on the hot skillet and grill it, turning every few minutes, until browned.

 6. While the sandwich cools a bit, decide where to bite first!

Creative Option:
For an extragooey sandwich, add a tomato slice before grilling.

HAM-STUFFED POTATOES

Potatoes—you may like them mashed, fried, and baked, but have you ever tried them stuffed with stuff? Try this ham filling, or use your imagination to make other winning and wonderful combinations.

Makes: 2 servings

Ingredients:
- 2 large potatoes
- ½ cup chopped ham
- ¼ cup grated Cheddar cheese
- 1 tablespoon sour cream
- 1 tablespoon chives, chopped
- Salt and pepper to taste

Materials:
- Oven
- Vegetable scrubber
- Fork
- Aluminum foil
- Oven mitts
- Measuring cups and spoons
- Mixing bowl
- Large spoon
- Sharp knife (for slicing)

What to Do:

 1. Preheat the oven to 400°F.

 2. **Scrub potatoes well.**

 3. Prick the potatoes with a fork.

4. **Wrap each potato separately in aluminum foil.**

 5. Use oven mitts to place the potatoes in the hot oven. Bake for 1 hour or until tender.

 6. While the potatoes are baking, combine the remaining ingredients in a bowl and mix well. Refrigerate until the potatoes are done.

 7. When the potatoes are done, carefully unwrap them and make a deep slice in the top of each.

 8. Spoon the ham mixture into the potatoes.

Creative Option:
Instead of ham, try cooked broccoli or spinach for a colorful and tasty variation.

PASTA-CHEESE SOUP

This recipe has a lot of ingredients and gives you a lot to do, but once it begins to simmer and you catch a whiff of it, you'll be jumping for joy. That's when the fun really begins!

Makes: 3 to 4 bowls

Ingredients:
- 2 cups canned chicken broth
- 2 green onions, chopped
- ½ cup dry shell pasta
- ½ cup pasteurized process cheese
- ¼ cup milk
- Salt and pepper to taste

Materials:
- Measuring cups
- Stove
- Large saucepan
- Large spoon
- Butter knife (for cutting)
- Serving bowls
- Ladle

What to Do:

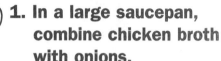

1. In a large saucepan, combine chicken broth with onions.

 2. Bring to a boil and stir in pasta; reduce heat to medium-low and cook for 6 to 7 minutes.

3. Use a butter knife to cut cheese into cubes.

4. Add cheese and milk to the broth and stir until the cheese melts.

 5. Ladle the soup into serving bowls.

 6. Sprinkle with salt and pepper.

Creative Option:
Sprinkle the soup with crunchy croutons or crisp cracker crumbs before serving.

PEANUT-BUTTER-AND-JELLY PINWHEELS

Everyone loves peanut butter and jelly, especially when it looks like this! These sandwiches are pretty enough to serve on any occasion.

Makes: 2 servings

Ingredients:
- 2 slices white sandwich bread
- Peanut butter
- Your favorite jam or jelly

Materials:
- Butter knife (for spreading)
- Toothpicks
- Plastic wrap
- Refrigerator

What to Do:

 1. Trim crusts from bread slices.

2. Spread a layer of peanut butter on each bread slice.

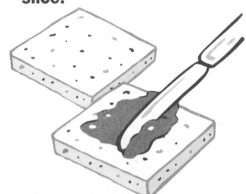

3. Spread a layer of jam on top of the peanut butter.

 4. Roll up each slice of bread.

 5. Secure each roll with a toothpick.

 6. Cover each roll tightly with plastic wrap and place in the refrigerator for a few minutes.

7. Remove toothpicks and cut each roll into slices.

8. **Arrange your pinwheels in a pretty pattern on a plate.**

Creative Option:
Try other combinations, like wheat bread with apple butter.

POTATO STICKS WITH RANCH DIP

Potato sticks with ranch dressing—if you haven't had these before, you have to try 'em. Just bake 'em up and chow down!

Makes: 2 servings

Ingredients:
- Vegetable-oil spray
- 2 potatoes, scrubbed
- 1 tablespoon vegetable oil
- Salt to taste
- Ranch dressing

Materials:
- Oven
- Cookie sheet
- Sharp knife (for slicing)
- Mixing bowls
- Measuring spoons
- Large spoon
- Oven mitts
- Serving plate
- Serving bowl

What to Do:

 1. Preheat the oven to 400°F.

 2. **Spray a cookie sheet with vegetable-oil spray.**

 3. Slice potatoes into long, thin sticks.

 4. **Put the potato sticks in a mixing bowl and sprinkle them with vegetable oil. Stir to coat.**

5. Lay the potatoes on the cookie sheet.

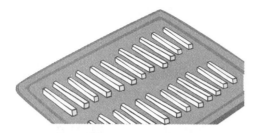

 6. Use oven mitts to place the potatoes in the hot oven. Bake for 20 minutes or until tender.

 7. Arrange the hot potato sticks on a serving plate and sprinkle them with salt.

 8. Pour some ranch dressing into a bowl and place in the middle of the potatoes for dipping.

Creative Option:
For extra zest, sprinkle ¼ cup grated cheese on oiled potatoes before baking.

SANDWICH ROUNDS

Round sandwiches just taste better; don't you agree? You'll love cutting out your own bread shapes and then biting into them. Experiment with different fillings to find your favorite!

Makes: 1 sandwich

Ingredients:
- 2 slices bread
- 1 tablespoon mayonnaise or soft cream cheese
- Cucumber slices, peeled
- Salt to taste

Materials:
- Cutting board
- Round cookie cutter
- Measuring spoons
- Butter knife (for spreading)

What to Do:

1. Place bread slices on a cutting board.

2. Use a round cookie cutter to cut each slice into a circle.

3. Spread one circle with mayonnaise or cream cheese.

4. Place cucumber slices on top of spread.

 6. Top with the other bread circle.

5. Sprinkle the cucumbers with salt.

Creative Options:
If you have fresh garden tomatoes, use them instead of cucumbers. Try some of these fillings as well: cheese slices and jam, peanut butter and mashed banana, or ham and mustard.

TUNA MELT

You won't have to fish for compliments when you serve these tasty tuna melts. Everyone will be asking for more of these terrific, toasty sandwiches. What a catch!

Makes: 4 servings

Ingredients:
- 1 6-ounce can tuna, drained
- 1–2 tablespoons sweet pickle relish
- 1 tablespoon mayonnaise
- 2 large French rolls, split
- 1 cup grated Swiss cheese

Materials:
- Oven
- Measuring spoons and cups
- Mixing bowl
- Fork
- Butter knife (for spreading)
- Cookie sheet
- Oven mitts

What to Do:

 1. Preheat the oven broiler.

 2. Put tuna, relish, and mayonnaise in a mixing bowl; mix well with a fork.

 3. Spread the tuna mixture onto cut sides of rolls.

4. **Place rolls faceup on a cookie sheet and sprinkle with cheese.**

5. Use oven mitts to place the baking sheet under the broiler. Heat until cheese is melted and bubbly.

6. **Wait until the tuna melts cool before eating!**

Creative Option:
Add chopped celery or grated carrot to the tuna mixture for more flavor and nutrition.

TURKEY WRAPPERS

You'll love the different flavors and textures in these turkey wrappers. Munch away, because these crunchy, tasty treats are good for you, too!

Makes: 2 servings
(2 wrappers per serving)

Ingredients:
- 4 pieces thinly sliced turkey
- 1 tablespoon mustard
- 1 celery stick, sliced into 4 thin strips

Materials:
- Measuring spoons
- Butter knife (for spreading)
- Plastic wrap or toothpicks
- Refrigerator

What to Do:

1. Lay turkey slices flat and spread with mustard.

2. Place a celery strip at one end of each turkey slice and roll it up.

3. Wrap each roll in plastic wrap or secure with a toothpick. Place in the refrigerator to chill for at least 30 minutes.

 4. **Remove plastic wrap or toothpicks and take a bite.**

Creative Option:
Experiment with different meats, spreads, and veggies. Try sliced roast beef with horseradish sauce and green pepper strips—mmm, peppy!

VEGGIE PITAS

Here's a lip-smacking way to get your veggies. Served up in a pita pocket, you can take this treat anywhere.

Makes: 2 servings (2 pita halves per serving)

Ingredients:
- ⅓ cup grated carrots
- ⅓ cup chopped green pepper
- ⅓ cup sliced mushrooms
- ⅓ cup sliced tomatoes
- 2 tablespoons salad dressing
- 2 pocket-style pita rounds
- 1 cup grated Swiss cheese

Materials:
- Measuring cups and spoons
- Large bowl
- Large spoon
- Sharp knife (for slicing)

What to Do:

 1. Place vegetables and salad dressing in a large bowl and mix.

 2. Cut each pita round in half and open pockets.

3. Spoon vegetable mixture into each pocket.

4. Sprinkle cheese into each pocket.

Creative Option:
If you want, you can add your favorite deli meat, such as turkey or ham.

WISH KEBABS

The great thing about these kebabs is that you can make them with whatever you wish! Take turns spearing different-colored foods to make de-wish-ous works of art. Who knew making lunch could be so fun?

Makes: as much as you want

Ingredients:
- Cheese chunks
- Ham or turkey pieces
- Cherry tomatoes
- Whole olives

Materials:
- Wooden skewers

What to Do:

 1. Arrange ingredients on the counter.

 2. **Spear the ingredients of your choice with the skewers, alternating colors to create pretty patterns.**

Creative Option:
Serve with ranch or honey mustard dressing for dipping.

SWEETS AND STUFF

AGGRESSION COOKIES

Do you ever feel so angry that you want to punch something? Try making these cookies to blow off some steam. Pounding on the dough will make you feel better, and the cookies taste great!

Makes: 36 cookies

Ingredients:
- 1½ cups butter or margarine, softened
- 1½ cups brown sugar
- 1½ cups flour
- 2 teaspoons baking soda
- 3 cups rolled oats
- 1 cup chocolate chips
- White sugar

Materials:
- Oven
- Measuring cups and spoons
- Large mixing bowl
- Cookie sheet
- Small juice glass
- Oven mitts and spatula
- Serving plate

What to Do:

 1. Preheat the oven to 350°F.

2. Place butter or margarine and brown sugar into a large mixing bowl and use your hands to squish them together.

3. Sift flour and baking soda into the dough. Mix well with your hands.

4. Add oats and chocolate chips and mix some more.

 5. Form the dough into 1-inch balls and place them on an ungreased cookie sheet.

Creative Options:
Try peanut-butter or butter-scotch chips instead of chocolate.

 6. Butter the bottom of a small glass and dip in white sugar. Mash the dough balls with the sugared glass. Reapply butter and sugar as needed.

 7. Use oven mitts to place the cookies in the hot oven. Bake for 10 to 12 minutes. Remove the cookies to a serving plate with a spatula.

 8. When the cookies are cool, eat 'em up!

CANDIED PRETZELS

It's easy to make your own candy with this quick pretzel dip. Each candied pretzel is a yummy work of art!

Makes: a big platter of pretzels

Ingredients:
- 6 ounces white chocolate
- 2 tablespoons light corn syrup
- 1 tablespoon milk
- 8 ounces pretzels
- Colored cookie sprinkles

Materials:
- Stove
- Small saucepan
- Measuring spoons
- Large spoon
- Wax paper
- Large plate
- Tongs
- Refrigerator
- Serving platter

What to Do:

 1. Melt chocolate in a small saucepan over low heat, then carefully stir in corn syrup and milk; mix until smooth.

 2. Remove the saucepan from heat.

 3. Spread a sheet of wax paper on a large plate placed near the saucepan.

4. Using tongs, dip pretzels into the hot chocolate.

 5. Lay the dipped pretzels on the wax paper and sprinkle with colored cookie sprinkles.

6. Place the plate in the refrigerator for about 20 minutes or until the chocolate is firm.

 7. Arrange the candied pretzels on a serving platter.

Creative Option:
Experiment with all kinds of pretzels: thin sticks, twists, and big logs.

CAROB-DIPPED STRAWBERRIES

A beautiful way to dress up strawberries—or any other favorite fruit—is to dip them in this candy coating. And, oh my—wait till you take a bite!

Makes: a plateful

Ingredients:
- 8 ounces carob chips (or in bar form, chopped)
- ½ pint fresh strawberries

Materials:
- Double boiler
- Large spoon
- Wax paper

What to Do:

 1. Melt carob chips in top of double boiler over hot water.

 2. Stir melted carob until it's smooth.

 3. Remove the melted carob from the heat.

 4. Spread wax paper out on the counter near the melted carob.

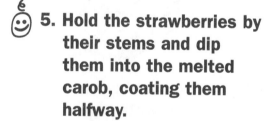

5. Hold the strawberries by their stems and dip them into the melted carob, coating them halfway.

6. Place on wax paper to set for about 2 hours.

Creative Options:
Semisweet-chocolate or white-chocolate chips also melt well for coating fruit.

CHERRY-OATMEAL BARS

Don't cry over spilled milk! Just pour another glass and grab a cherry-oatmeal bar to go with it. These bars are chewy and wholesome, and they go great with a tall glass of you-know-what.

Makes: 9 large bars

Ingredients:
- ½ cup butter or margarine, softened
- ⅓ cup sugar
- 1 cup flour
- 1 cup rolled oats
- 1 21-ounce can cherry pie filling

Materials:
- Oven
- Measuring cups
- 2 mixing bowls
- 2 large spoons
- 9-inch-square baking dish
- Sharp knife (for slicing)
- Oven mitts
- Spatula
- Serving plates

What to Do:

1. Preheat the oven to 400°F.

2. **In a large mixing bowl, stir together butter or margarine and sugar.**

3. **Combine flour and oats in a separate bowl and add to the butter mixture. Mix until well blended.**

4. **Press half of the mixture in the bottom of a 9-inch-square baking dish.**

5. **Spoon pie filling over the dough.**

6. Spread the remaining oat mixture over the cherry filling. Use oven mitts to place the pan into the hot oven. Bake for 20 to 25 minutes or until browned. Cool a little before slicing into bars.

7. **Use a spatula to put a bar on your plate.**

Creative Option:
You can use any flavor of pie filling; blueberry and apple are delicious, too!

CHOCOLATE-CHIP SQUARES

Wait till you try this treat! Chewy and chock-full of chocolate chips, these squares are so good, they're sure to become your family's favorite.

Makes: 16 squares

Ingredients:
- 1 stick butter
- 1½ cups graham-cracker crumbs
- ½ cup flaked coconut
- 1 cup chocolate chips
- 1 can sweetened condensed milk

Materials:
- Oven
- Microwave-safe bowl
- Microwave
- 8-inch-square baking pan
- Measuring cups
- Large spoon
- Oven mitts
- Sharp knife (for slicing)

What to Do:

 1. Preheat the oven to 350°F.

  2. **Place a stick of butter into a microwave-safe bowl.**

 3. Place the bowl in the microwave and heat for 1 minute on high.

4. Remove the bowl from the microwave and pour the melted butter into the baking pan.

5. Sprinkle graham-cracker crumbs on top of the butter and use a large spoon to spread them evenly.

6. Spoon flaked coconut on top of the crumbs.

 **7. Spread chocolate chips over the coconut, then pour a can of sweetened condensed milk over all.**

 8. Use oven mitts to place the pan into the hot oven. Bake 35 minutes, then let cool. Slice into squares.

9. Enjoy!

Creative Option:
If you don't like coconut, just leave it out. The squares will still be scrumptious.

CINNAMON CRISPS

When you're in the mood for something sweet, crisp, and sensational, these cinnamon crisps will fill the bill. Try them and see if you don't agree!

Makes: 1 serving

Ingredients:
- 1 tablespoon margarine
- 1 flour tortilla
- ½ teaspoon cinnamon
- 1 teaspoon sugar

Materials:
- Oven
- Measuring spoons
- Microwave-safe bowl
- Microwave
- Cutting board
- Sharp knife (for slicing)
- Cookie sheet
- Pastry brush
- Oven mitts

What to Do:

 1. Preheat the oven to 350°F.

 2. **Put the margarine in a microwave-safe bowl.**

3. Place the bowl in the microwave and heat for 1 minute on high.

4. Remove the bowl from the microwave.

5. **Lay the tortilla flat on a cutting board.**

 6. Cut the tortilla into four wedges.

 7. **Place the wedges on a cookie sheet.**

 8. **Use a pastry brush to spread melted margarine over the tortilla wedges.**

 9. **Sprinkle the tortilla wedges with cinnamon and sugar.**

 10. Use oven mitts to place the tortilla wedges in the hot oven. Bake for 20 minutes or until golden and crisp.

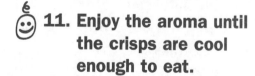 11. **Enjoy the aroma until the crisps are cool enough to eat.**

Creative Option:
For a taste that's twice as nice, try dipping the crisps in applesauce.

FRUIT PIZZA

Makes: 8 to 10 servings

Ingredients:
- Vegetable-oil spray
- 20 ounces refrigerated sugar-cookie dough
- 8 ounces cream cheese, softened
- ½ cup sugar
- 1 teaspoon vanilla
- ½ cup sliced strawberries
- ½ cup sliced kiwi
- ½ cup pineapple chunks
- ½ cup blueberries
- ½ cup orange marmalade
- 2 tablespoons water

Materials:
- Oven
- Round pizza pan
- Oven mitts
- Measuring cups and spoons
- Large mixing bowl
- Electric mixer
- Butter knife (for spreading)
- Small bowl
- Fork
- Sharp knife (for slicing)

What to Do:

 1. Preheat the oven to 350°F.

 2. Spray a round pizza pan with vegetable-oil spray.

3. Spread cookie dough evenly in the pan. Use oven mitts to place the pan in the hot oven. Bake for 10 to 12 minutes or until golden brown. Let cool.

 4. Place cream cheese, sugar, and vanilla in a large mixing bowl.

5. Beat with an electric mixer until well blended.

 6. Spread the cream-cheese mixture over the baked crust.

 7. Arrange fruit in a pretty pattern on top of the cream cheese.

 8. In a small bowl, use a fork to mix marmalade with water. Drizzle the marmalade mixture over fruit, refrigerate 30 minutes to set, then slice into serving-size wedges.

9. Enjoy your fruity pizza!

Creative Option:
Top your pizza with any fruits you like: Raspberries, grapes, cherries, and sliced peaches all work well.

GRAHAM-CRACKER DUNKER DIP

Who doesn't like peanut butter? If you're tired of peanut-butter sandwiches, here's a new way to enjoy your favorite flavor. Grab a handful of crackers and take a dip! Happy dunking!

Makes: 2 to 4 servings

Ingredients:
- 1 cup peanut-butter chips
- 2 tablespoons milk
- Graham crackers

Materials:
- Measuring cups and spoons
- Double boiler
- Large spoon
- Small serving bowl

What to Do:

 1. Place peanut-butter chips and milk in top of double boiler and melt.

 2. **Stir the mixture until it's smooth.**

 3. Remove the peanut-butter mixture from the heat.

😊 **4. Spoon the peanut-butter mixture into a small serving bowl.**

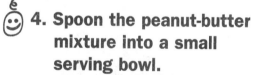

😊 **5. Grab a cracker and go for a dip!**

Creative Options:
See how may yummy things you can come up with for dunking. How about animal crackers or pretzels? Banana chunks or apple slices? Celery sticks or rice cakes?

MICROWAVE S'MORES

What's sweet and gooey and oh-so-good? Why, s'mores, of course! "S'more" is short for "some more," which is exactly what you'll shout after you try this treat!

Makes: 1 serving

Ingredients:
- 2 graham-cracker squares
- 1 square of a chocolate candy bar
- 1 large marshmallow

Materials:
- Paper towels
- Microwave

What to Do:

 1. Place a paper towel on the counter.

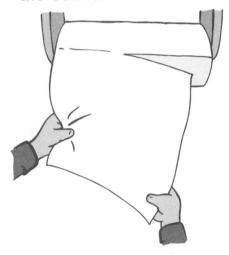

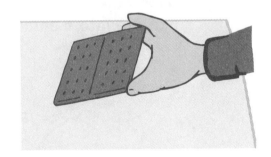 2. Place one graham cracker on the paper towel.

3. Place a chocolate square and a large marshmallow on top of the cracker.

 4. Top with the other graham cracker.

5. Wrap the s'more in the paper towel.

6. Place the wrapped s'more in the microwave and heat on high for 10 to 20 seconds or until the marshmallow puffs up.

7. Let the s'more cool a bit before you gobble it up.

Creative Option:
Chocolate chips with marshmallow cream work well, too!

PEANUT-BUTTER-AND-JELLY COOKIES

These cookies are so tasty, they'll disappear in no time!

Makes: 36 cookies

Ingredients:
- Vegetable-oil spray
- 1 cup granulated sugar
- 1 cup brown sugar
- 1 cup butter
- 1 cup peanut butter
- 2 eggs
- 2¼ cups flour
- 2 teaspoons baking soda
- ¼ teaspoon salt
- 1 teaspoon vanilla
- 1 cup strawberry jam

Materials:
- Oven
- Cookie sheet
- Measuring cups and spoons
- Large mixing bowl
- Electric mixer
- Sifter
- Large spoon
- Oven mitts
- Spatula and plate

What to Do:

 1. Preheat the oven to 350°F.

 2. **Spray a cookie sheet with vegetable-oil spray.**

 3. In a large mixing bowl, beat sugars, butter, and peanut butter with an electric mixer.

 4. **Add eggs to the butter mixture.**

5. Beat the mixture until it's well blended.

6. Sift flour, baking soda, and salt into the mixture. Add vanilla and stir.

7. Roll the dough into balls and flatten slightly.

8. Place the flattened balls on the cookie sheet.

 9. Press a teaspoon into the center of each cookie to form a well.

10. Use oven mitts to place the cookies in the hot oven. Bake for 8 to 10 minutes or until golden. Then transfer the cookies with a spatula to a plate.

11. While the cookies are still warm, fill each well with a teaspoon of jam.

Creative Option:
Just about any jelly or jam will work. Grape jelly and plum jam are great!

PUDDING PARFAITS

Who says pudding has to be boring? Tempt your taste buds with this dreamy dessert. It's as fun to look at as it is to eat!

Makes: 4 servings

Ingredients:
- 2 cups cold milk
- 3.4-ounce box instant pudding mix (any flavor)
- 2–3 cups whipped topping

Materials:
- Measuring cups
- Large mixing bowl
- Electric mixer
- Large spoon
- 4 wine glasses or parfait dishes
- 2 spoons

What to Do:

1. Pour milk into a large mixing bowl.

2. Add instant pudding mix.

3. Use an electric mixer to beat pudding and milk for 2 minutes.

4. **Alternately spoon layers of pudding and whipped topping into wineglasses or parfait dishes.**

5. **Finish the parfait with a dab of whipped topping.**

Creative Options:
Decorate your parfaits with candy sprinkles, or garnish each with a cherry.

SHERBET SNOWBALLS

Have a ball—a snowball, that is! These snowballs are for eating—not throwing—and you can make them all year 'round. They taste especially good in the summer!

Makes: as many as you like

Ingredients:
- Coconut flakes
- Any flavor of sherbet

Materials:
- 2 large plates
- Aluminum foil
- Ice-cream scoop
- Freezer
- Plastic freezer bag

What to Do:

1. Pour coconut onto a large plate.

2. Cover a second plate with aluminum foil.

3. Use an ice-cream scoop to make round balls of sherbet.

 4. Roll the balls in coconut and place them on the foil-covered plate.

 5. Place the plate in the freezer for about 1 hour or until the snowballs are hard. Store in a freezer bag to prevent freezer burn.

6. Thaw the snowballs slightly before eating them.

Creative Option:
Make "dirty" snowballs by rolling sherbet in chocolate sprinkles or carob chips instead of coconut.

STUFFED APPLE BAKE

They say an apple a day keeps the doctor away. If you eat an apple every day, it's nice to prepare it in a different way. Try this recipe for baked apples. You won't believe how good they smell and taste!

Makes: 2 servings

Ingredients:
- 2 apples
- 2 tablespoons raisins
- 1 tablespoon brown sugar
- 1 tablespoon margarine
- 1 teaspoon cinnamon
- 1 cup apple juice

Materials:
- Sharp knife (for slicing)
- Microwave-safe dish
- Mixing bowl
- Measuring spoons and cups
- Large spoon
- Microwave
- 2 plates

What to Do:

1. Cut apples in half and scoop out the cores.

2. Place the hollowed-out apples in a microwave-safe dish.

3. In a mixing bowl, combine raisins, brown sugar, margarine, and cinnamon.

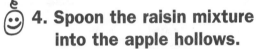

4. Spoon the raisin mixture into the apple hollows.

5. Pour apple juice over the apples.

6. Place the apples in the microwave and heat them for 4 minutes on high. When the apples are tender, remove them from the microwave.

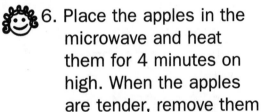

7. Get two plates ready for one of the best treats you'll ever have!

Creative Option:
If you want your baked apples to be really fancy, top them with a dollop of sour cream or whipped cream.

SUPER SUNDAE

Here's the scoop: This recipe uses chocolate sauce and fruit for toppings, but you can make your sundae any way you want. Whatever toppings you choose, you're in for a treat!

Makes: 2 servings

Ingredients:
- 2 scoops frozen yogurt
- 2 tablespoons chocolate sauce
- ½ cup raspberries

Materials:
- 2 dessert cups
- Ice-cream scoop
- Measuring spoons and cups

What to Do:

 1. Put a scoop of yogurt in each dessert cup.

 2. **Drizzle chocolate sauce over the yogurt and top with raspberries.**

Creative Option:
Caramel sauce and chopped nuts also make great toppings.

DELICIOUS DRINKS

BANANA SMOOTHIE

Tempt your taste buds with an energy-boosting banana smoothie. Full of fruit and milk, this drink is fast, easy, and good for you. Chug-a-lug!

Makes: 1 glass

Ingredients:
- 1 cup milk
- 1 banana, sliced
- 1 teaspoon honey
- 3 ice cubes

Materials:
- Blender
- Measuring cups and spoons
- Tall glass

What to Do:

1. Pour milk into a blender.

2. Add banana slices and honey.

 3. Blend the milk, banana, and honey until smooth.

 4. Add ice cubes to the banana mixture.

 5. Blend the mixture again until it's smooth.

 6. Pour the mixture into a tall glass.

 7. Drink it up!

Creative Option:
Use frozen fruit instead of a banana and skip the ice cubes.

CHOCOLATE ICE-CREAM SODA

The chocolate. The fizz. Explore the wonders of your very own chocolate ice-cream soda. You'll get to the bottom of this in no time!

Makes: 1 glass

Ingredients:
- 1 scoop chocolate ice cream
- ¼ cup milk
- Club soda

Materials:
- Ice-cream scoop
- Tall glass
- Measuring cups
- 2 long spoons
- 2 straws

What to Do:

1. Place a scoop of ice cream in a tall glass.

2. **Pour milk over the ice cream.**

3. **Fill the glass to the top with club soda.**

4. Set out two long spoons, put two straws in the glass, and drink up!

Creative Option:
If you're a real chocoholic, add a squirt of chocolate syrup.

CINNAMON CIDER

What's better than a piping-hot cup of apple cider? A cup of cider flavored with cinnamon candies! While you're waiting for the cider to cool, sit back and enjoy the cinnamon aroma steaming from the cups.

Makes: 2 servings

Ingredients:
- 2 cups apple cider
- 2 tablespoons cinnamon candies

Materials:
- Measuring cups and spoons
- Saucepan
- Stove
- Spoon
- 2 mugs

Creative Option:
Use a cinnamon stick as a stirrer or a straw.

What to Do:

 1. Pour apple cider into a saucepan.

 2. Cook over medium heat until hot (but not boiling). Stir in cinnamon candies until melted. Pour the cider into mugs.

 3. Wait a bit until the cider cools enough to drink. Then sip away!

COCOA DELIGHT

Who needs instant cocoa when it's just as easy to make the real thing? This simple, scrumptious drink is sure to delight you. It'll warm your hands and your heart at the same time!

Makes: 4 servings

Ingredients:
- ⅓ cup cocoa
- ⅓ cup white sugar
- ¼ teaspoon salt
- ½ cup water
- 3½ cups milk

Materials:
- Measuring cups and spoons
- Large saucepan
- Stove
- Spoon
- 4 mugs

Creative Option:
Sprinkle a bit of cinnamon in each mug for cocoa with a Mexican flair.

What to Do:

 1. **Put the cocoa, sugar, salt, and water in a large saucepan. Mix well.**

 2. Stir the mixture over medium-high heat until it boils.

 3. Reduce the heat and add milk. Stir until hot, then turn off the heat and pour the cocoa into mugs.

 4. **Hug your mug and chug-a-lug!**

PINK LEMONADE

When a long day at the playground has left you high and dry, there's nothing better than a tall glass of tart and tasty lemonade.

Makes: 2 glasses

Ingredients:
- 2 lemons
- ¼ cup sugar
- 2 cups water
- 2 tablespoons maraschino cherry juice
- 6 ice cubes
- 2 maraschino cherries

Materials:
- Sharp knife (for slicing)
- Cutting board
- Hand juicer
- Strainer
- Pitcher
- Measuring cups and spoons
- Long spoon
- 2 tall glasses

What to Do:

 1. Cut lemons in half on a cutting board.

2. Press and twist each lemon half on the juicer to squeeze out the juice.

3. Pour the lemon juice into a pitcher through a strainer to remove seeds.

4. Add sugar, water, and cherry juice, and mix well.

5. Place three ice cubes in each glass and pour lemonade over the ice.

6. Top each glass with a cherry.

Creative Option:
Use club soda instead of water for fizzy lemonade.

RASPBERRY PUNCH

This pink punch is pretty enough for a party—or for when you just need a special pick-me-up. You're sure to find it absolutely delectable!

Makes: 1 glass

Ingredients:
- 1 scoop raspberry sherbet
- ½ cup cranberry juice
- ½ cup ginger ale

Materials:
- Ice-cream scoop
- Tall glass
- Measuring cups
- Long spoon
- Drinking straw

What to Do:

 1. Place a scoop of sherbet in a tall glass.

2. **Pour cranberry juice over the sherbet.**

3. **Fill the glass to the top with ginger ale.**

4. Plunk a long spoon and a straw into the glass, and sip your fizzy punch.

Creative Option:
For a different taste, try lime sherbet with white grape juice. It's irresistible!

ROOT-BEER FLOAT

No wonder this old favorite is still so popular: Everyone likes root beer and ice cream, and together they're twice as nice! Stir up your own root-beer float for a good taste and a good time.

Makes: 1 large mugful

Ingredients:
- 2 scoops vanilla ice cream
- 1 can root beer

Materials:
- 1 large glass mug
- Freezer
- Ice-cream scoop
- Long spoon

What to Do:

 1. About 30 minutes before making your root-beer float, place a large glass mug in the freezer.

 2. Take the cold, frosty mug out of the freezer.

 3. Place two scoops of ice cream into the frosty mug.

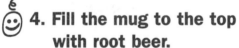 4. Fill the mug to the top with root beer.

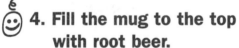 5. Grab a long spoon and enjoy an old-fashioned treat!

Creative Option:
Use your imagination and combine any of your favorite carbonated sodas with a variety of ice-cream flavors.

STRAWBERRY-YOGURT SHAKE

Jammed full of fruit and crammed full of yogurt . . . how much healthier can you get? For breakfast or for bedtime, give this shake a whirl!

Makes: 2 servings

Ingredients:
- 1 cup milk
- 1 cup strawberries, fresh or frozen
- 1 cup strawberry yogurt

Materials:
- Measuring cups
- Blender
- 2 glasses

What to Do:

1. Pour milk into a blender.

2. Add strawberries.

3. Blend the milk and strawberries until smooth.

 4. Add strawberry yogurt to the milk mixture.

 5. Blend at low speed for 1 or 2 minutes until creamy.

 6. **Pour the mixture into two glasses and gulp down your simply splendid shakes!**

Creative Option:
Use any fruit and yogurt combinations that you like!

TROPICAL SLUSHIES

What's really cool on a hot summer day? These tropical slushies: They're frosty, fruity, and fun!

Makes: 4 slushies

Ingredients:
- 2 bananas
- ¼ cup lemon juice
- 1 cup orange juice
- 1 6-ounce can crushed pineapple
- 2 12-ounce cans lemon-lime soda

Materials:
- Large mixing bowl
- Fork
- Measuring cups
- Spoon
- Plastic bowl
- Freezer
- Ice-cream scoop
- 4 tall glasses
- 4 long spoons

What to Do:

1. Peel bananas and place them in a large bowl. Mash the bananas with a fork.

2. Add lemon juice, orange juice, and pineapple. Stir well.

3. Pour the mixture into a plastic bowl, cover, and freeze for a couple of hours until firm. When ready to serve, thaw slightly to a slushy consistency.

 4. Scoop several spoonfuls of slush into each glass with an ice-cream scoop.

 5. Fill the glasses to the top with lemon-lime soda.

 6. Grab a long spoon and dig in!

Creative Option:
Add maraschino cherries before freezing for more color!

ZIPPY ORANGE FIZZ

This simple recipe is a supereasy and superswell way to dress up your orange juice. Watch it bubble up, then take a swig. Bottoms up!

Makes: as much as you want

Ingredients:
- 2 parts orange juice
- 1 part club soda or ginger ale

Materials:
- Drinking glasses
- Drinking straws

What to Do:

1. Fill each glass about ⅔ full of orange juice.

2. Add club soda or ginger ale and watch it fizz. Drink with a straw.

Creative Option:
Garnish each glass with an orange slice.

HAVE FUN!

Isn't cooking fun? Now that you've learned how to make all these yummy treats, you'll want to invite your friends and family to share them. You may even be ready to try some new recipes or get creative and do things differently with some of your old favorites.

There's just no limit to what you can do now that you've learned your way around the kitchen. Just remember: Be careful and have fun!

MOMMY'S LITTLE HELPER CHRISTMAS CRAFTS

by Cynthia MacGregor
Illustrated by Glenn Quist

Now children can deck the halls with crafts they've made themselves (with just a little help from Mom). Each project comes with easy-to-follow illustrated instructions for the child. There are directions for Mom, too!

While Mom takes care of tasks that need scissors, craft knives, and needles, the child gets to tear, paste, draw, and glue. These 40 creative crafts are guaranteed to help kids and parents enjoy the holidays with crafts that celebrate the spirit of Christmas.

Order #2445 $8.00

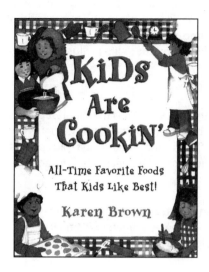

KIDS ARE COOKIN'

by Karen Brown
Illustrated by Laurel Aiello

Here are 100 all-time-favorite, kid-pleasing recipes for everything from snacks and drinks to entrées and desserts. These are the recipes that kids like best, passed on from one generation to the next, written in a style that makes cooking fun for kids.

Order #2440 $8.00

KIDS' PARTY COOKBOOK

by Penny Warner
Illustrated by Laurel Aiello

Over 175 reduced-fat recipes with food that's fun and tasty for kids, but full of nutrition to please parents. Warner has fun ideas for every meal, including mini-meals, such as Peanut Butter Burger Dogs and Twinkle Sandwiches; creative snacks, such as Aquarium Jello and Prehistoric Bugs; nutritious drinks, such as Beetle Juice and Apple Jazz; creative desserts, such as Spaghetti Ice Cream and Doll-in-the-Cake; holiday fare, such as Candy Cane Parfaits for Christmas and Jack O' Lantern Custard for Halloween.

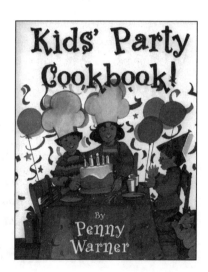

Order #2435 $12.00